Teddy Saves the Day

by Max Aron

illustrated by Le Uyen Pham

On Monday, Teddy was in class.

"How do things move?" Miss Meadow asked.

"Some things move when you push them," said Teddy.

"That's right," said Miss Meadow.

"Some things move when you pull them," said Teddy.

On Tuesday, Teddy heard Pam shout.

"My doll fell into the water," Pam shouted.

The doll's head was all wet. Teddy pulled her out.

Teddy saved the day!

On Wednesday, Teddy
heard Matt shout.

Matt shouted, "The glue
spilled all over the table."

Mouse was going into
the glue. Teddy pushed
Mouse away.

Teddy saved the day!

On Thursday, Teddy heard Kate shout.

"Someone shut the door on Rabbit," Kate shouted.

Teddy rushed to pull open the door.

Teddy saved the day!

Now it was Friday.

"Perhaps I will
never save the day
again," Teddy said sadly.

He put his head down.
Then he heard some
laughter.

Ben had thrown the ball to Pam. But the ball had hit the vacuum. The ball had turned on the vacuum! The toys were going to be sucked in!

Teddy ran over to the vacuum. He had never run so fast. He pulled the vacuum out of the way.

Teddy saved the day!
He should win a prize!

Comprehension Check

Retell the Story

Use a Problem and Solution Chart to retell the story.

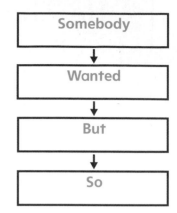

Think and Compare

1. What problem does Teddy solve on Friday? How does he solve it?

2. Tell about a problem you solved in school. What did you do?

3. Name two things you can push and two things you can pull.